Look what I made

Emerald Garcia - Finnis

BookLeaf Publishing

Presentation by *BookLeaf Publishing*

Web: www.bookleafpub.com

E-mail: info@bookleafpub.com

ISBN: 9789357445566

First edition 2022

DEDICATION

For

Mami & Papi,

Gram Gram

Grandma and Grandpa

I finally did the thing.

PREFACE

These poems aren't directed at anyone in
particular.
If you see yourself here,
perhaps you owe me an apology.

or, alternatively
I love you too.

For Want of the Sun

In want of the sun,

I opened myself

To bask in its abundance.

To absorb the warm honeyed glow

And feel the trickle of serotonin

Flow through the very core of my being.

In want of the sun,

I allowed myself to inhale

The crisp possibilities of a blinding future

Wherein, I would transcend

Into the highest form of myself

And awaken my life's purpose

In want of the sun,

I convinced myself so surprisingly well

That I could make it happen

That it would come as

easily as that first deep inhale

In want of the sun,

I spread my reach across the sky

Trying to recreate the image in my minds

I, have grown tired and disheartened

from the pursuit

And so, I planted roots in the mundane

In want of the sun,

I never learned to exhale

And now I choke

on the sharp jagged edges

Of wasted potential

That has taken seed in my lungs

In want of the sun,

A shadow was cast

And I made my home in the dark.

Golden

Do not ask

The beautiful black woman

Where she is from

She does not owe you

An explanation

For her radiance

Simply admire the glow.

Midnight wish

5

When I asked the universe for you

I wasn't really expecting an answer

And little did I know, but

You were much more than what I asked for

Unrest

'Are you okay?'

'I' am fine

But there is unrest in my spirit

My heart is weighed down so much I fear it

Will catch inside my chest

And squeeze the air from my lungs

My throat stings as though I have

Spent a lifetime singing their name

In hopes they would come back again

The silence is deafening

But even still

The swirl of voices within won't

Let me fill my mind

With anything but old memory reel

But this is my burden to feel

And so, I say

'I' am fine

From your point of view

I never really liked my eyes

They weren't as deep blue as the ocean

And they didn't shift in the sun

to match the temperament of the sky

No matter how I perceived them

They were always just

Brown

But you loved my eyes

And I loved

The way you looked

Into mine

If I wrote the way
that I think

If I wrote the way that I think

My fingertips would be stained

By the sea of ink gushing

From every

Relentless,

Dissecting,

Thought

I'd have manuscripts of manic scrawl

Sprawled across my floors

I'd have spiraling towers of paper

Cataloguing each

Erratic,

Convoluted,

Sequence

of my nervous breakdowns

And

I'd have entire libraries

Filled

Wholly,

Unreservedly

of you

A Gift

A rare find indeed

Some minor imperfections

Most valuable

The hardest part

The hardest part

Of being the strong one

Is that you spend

so long

Saving yourself

That you assume

you are the only one

who can.

When I think of

home

Piano

Egg Hunt

First Snow

Beef Patties

Sunday Service

Checkered Tiles

Cheerleading

Praise Dance

Hubba Bubba

Airplane

VHS

Fall

Barrettes

Wildberry

Kart wheels

Big Slice Pops

Pigs In A Blanket

Chicken and Dumplings

Merry Go Round

Ferris Wheel

Stinky Boo

Glasses

Trilby

Floaties

Halloween

Front Steps

Roller Skates

Night Gowns

Bunk Beds

Pumpkin

Beads

Decisions

Feelings could never be wrong

They are but our deepest desires

Born on the skin

It is in the action of those feelings

That show us who we are

And leave the lasting scars

Warm Sheets

As loud a high-heels on early morning streets

As raw as conversations in parked cars

As gentle as forehead kisses and back tickles

As comforting as a mug of chai tea

As wholesome as a postcard in the mail

As entertaining as nights with no sleep

As all-consuming as a cocoon of warm sheets

You will always have my love

She's so clever

The kinky coils

A testament

to the relentless struggle

to embrace

the strength and beauty

that has been gifted to me

Her existence

defiant and unruly

in her naturalness

and so

she is concealed in plain sight

Each ebony strand

painstakingly poised

as though they themselves

embody the flow

of rivers and roads

Every inch of my crown

is weft into a tapestry

depicting generations of excellence

passed down in its very core

But you cannot fathom

having been blessed

with a gift such as this

And pronounce absently

PSA

I definitely don't say it enough

And please don't call my bluff

But I don't know what I'd do

If I didn't have you

But I imagine going through life would be rough.

Unmasked

I wasn't myself

for months

And no one noticed

All except for you.

What if?

If I never met you

I could have gone

my entire life

In blissful ignorance

Nothing would be amiss

Except

For a deeper longing

for something

I cannot name

Thankfully

I won't have to wonder

For long

Because I did

And it's been amazing.

24

Juggling

Unfortunately

My brain has many things to hold

And still

No pockets

With time

I can't recall when it started

But I realised you were right

It does get easier

Not all at once, but

in unrecognisable increments

Until one day

You exhale

And it too

is gone

Goodluck

To the girl with unwavering ambition

Who devoured books as though they alone

Breathed life into her body

Who accepted any challenge

In spite of the fear that would prickle her skin

And cause her stomach to swirl

Who dreamt openly and willfully

Of where she would be

at this time and place

I'm inclined to say

I'm sorry

The road that we had mapped out

Has long lost its tracks

And I am definitely too stubborn

To navigate back

But I am happy to report

We got a couple things right

And he is wishing you Goodluck tonight.

I still remember

I should have told you

You have always felt like home

Please don't ever doubt

Friendly Fire

One of these days

I will realise

That I am the only one

Rooting against me

And I will learn to stop

Breaking my own heart

Five more minutes

Just five more minutes

And I will rise from my bed

Ready to take on

the day ahead

In four more minutes

I'll awaken for sure

But not a minute earlier

Dare I stir

With three more minutes

I'll be fully renewed

And slink into the kitchen

In search of food

Not two more minutes

And I'll actually have to go

I really really

Don't want to though

At one more minute

I will open my eyes

And oh my

What a lovely surprise

I am late for work

www.ingramcontent.com/pod-product-compliance
Lightning Source LLC
La Vergne TN
LVHW010937200726
843509LV00013B/2237